Kim, ♡

My Girl. Thank you
for being my rock.
My Constant. I love ya
forever & Always.

Kevyn

10/26/21

GLACIER
unforgettable

Foreword by Chris Peterson

PHOTOGRAPHY BY CHUCK HANEY

FARCOUNTRY
PRESS

ISBN: 978-1-56037-516-6

For more information about our books, write Farcountry Press, P.O. Box 5630, Helena, MT 59604;
call (800) 821-3874; or visit www.farcountrypress.com.

Produced in the United States of America.
Printed in China.

19 18 17 16 15   2 3 4 5 6

Above: A panoramic view of Elizabeth and Helen lakes as seen from near the Ptarmigan Tunnel.

Right: A modest, two-mile round-trip hike takes visitors to spectacular Apikuni Falls in Many Glacier. There are more than 125 waterfalls in Glacier National Park.

Title page: Dusty Star Mountain is bathed in glorious early-morning light on Glacier's east side.

Cover: As the snow melts at Logan Pass, an enchanted landscape of glacier lilies blooms beneath the horn of Mount Reynolds.

Back cover: Baring Creek rushes to St. Mary Lake as first light strikes Going-to-the-Sun Mountain, left, and Matahpi Peak.

Jackson Glacier is one of only a few glaciers in the park that are visible from the road. An overlook just off Going-to-the-Sun Road on the park's east side gives visitors a long-distance view of the glacier, as well as Jackson Peak. At 10,052 feet, Jackson is one of six peaks in the park that surpass 10,000 feet.

FOREWORD | *By Chris Peterson*

Photographer Chuck Haney has been coming to Glacier National Park for twenty years now.

It has become a wonderful ailment—or, perhaps more fittingly, a cure.

"The park gets in your blood," he explains. "You never know what you'll find around the next corner. It keeps pulling me back. It's like home."

This home is a magical landscape of more than 1 million acres—sculpted by wind, massaged by rain, blanketed by snow, and scorched by fire. Even in the worst weather, the beauty, unfettered and unfiltered, seeps through.

Glacier's mountains aren't particularly high by mountain standards; the park's tallest peak, Mount Cleveland at the north end of the park, is only 10,466 feet high. But it's the drama of the sheer, jutting peaks between deep, glacially carved valleys that defines the awesome views in Glacier National Park.

Much of the rock is ancient seabed, more than a billion years old, lifted to the heavens by a restless continent and then worn into valleys, lakes, and gorges by the massive power of glaciers. However, the namesake features of this park are rapidly disappearing. In the mid-1800s, the park had about 150 glaciers. Today, about 25 remain. By 2030, geologists estimate they'll all be gone.

Archaeological evidence suggests that people first came to this area more than 8,000 years ago. Over the millennia, many American Indian tribes have lived in these mountains, but the two that have had the longest presence here—more than 1,000 years—are the Blackfeet and the Kutenai.

The rich resources of the northern Rocky Mountains began drawing fur traders from the East and from Europe in the 1700s, and in 1889 the Great Northern Railway reached the base of the Rockies. Tourists started arriving within a few short years, and on May 11, 1910, Glacier became the tenth national park in the United States. Soon came construction of the great lodges: Glacier Park Lodge, Many Glacier Hotel, Lake McDonald Lodge, and Waterton's Prince of Wales Hotel—as well as the backcountry Granite Park and Sperry chalets. In 1932 Glacier joined Waterton Lakes National Park in Canada to become Waterton–Glacier International Peace Park.

By the mid-1920s, the automobile had overtaken the horse and railroad as the mode of transportation by which to explore the West. Park officials decided to construct a fifty-mile road across the Continental Divide over a rugged and unforgiving route. Construction of the alpine section of the Going-to-the Sun Road began in the mid-1920s and was completed in the fall of 1932. The road—a marvel of engineering—opened to the public the summer of 1933, connecting West Glacier with St. Mary and becoming one of the most magnificent highways in North America.

The Going-to-the-Sun Road is marked by hairpin turns, hand-hewn stone masonry, and sheer white-knuckle cliffs. It is, by far, the most popular drive in Glacier National Park and, for many, its most popular attraction.

But the bulk of the park is swathed in solitude. Although an average of about 2 million people visit Glacier each year, much of the park is wilderness and is managed as such. Nearly every animal species that the Lewis and Clark Expedition documented during their journey through this part of the Rockies in 1806 is still here today.

The park is home to black and grizzly bears, mountain lions, lynx, bobcats, wolves, bighorn sheep, mountain goats, mule deer, white-tailed deer, elk, moose, and even wolverine, to name a few. Even the casual visitor has a chance to see many of the creatures on the list, particularly in the summer months.

Glacier is a hiker's paradise. It has more than 730 miles of maintained trails, 1,514 miles of perennial streams, 131 named lakes, 185 named peaks, 631 unnamed lakes, and countless waterfalls. Hikers, through a permit system, can stay at any number of backcountry primitive campgrounds and get away from it all—quite literally. Refreshingly and delightfully, there is virtually no cell phone service in the park.

The park's dramatic topography defines its regions and boundaries. A designated Wild and Scenic River, the North Fork of the Flathead makes up Glacier's western boundary. The region is one of unspoiled beauty, of mirror-like lakes, and of graceful prairies that butt up against the massive peaks that make up the Continental Divide. The North Fork also has no paved roads, save for the Camas Road, which is closed in the winter.

Water sculpts the rocks of Avalanche Gorge. It's a magical and short boardwalk stroll (less than one mile) through giant cedars and cottonwoods to the gorge. Many hikers continue to Avalanche Lake, so named because in the spring, avalanches cascade off the surrounding cliffs, sometimes tumbling all the way to the lakeshore.

Glacier's southern boundary is equally primitive. Although U.S. Highway 2, the Middle Fork of the Flathead River, and the railroad both run alongside the southern border, the southern portion of the park has no roads. The often overlooked area between Marias Pass and West Glacier is characterized by deep old-growth forests, trails that run for days rather than miles, and a permanent sense of quiet.

Glacier's east side is decidedly different than the west. Battered by the wind, an old-growth tree here might only be as big around as your arm. Here, the valley floor is a mile high. The vast prairies of Blackfeet country seem to crash into the steep and rugged divide. There are paved roads into the Two Medicine, St. Mary, and Many Glacier valleys. The landscape is rich with wildlife, and the weather can change on the breath of a butterfly, going from a sun-drenched afternoon to snow in a matter of hours.

In Glacier's northernmost region, on the east side, flows the Belly River. A backcountry paradise, accessible only by foot, it is the ultimate in wildness. With acres of lush meadows, peaks that look like the fingers of a giant reaching through the crust of the earth toward the sky, and two pristine rivers filled with fish, the northern section seems like a place untouched by time.

Glacier is a land of dreams within dreams. Memories within memories. Shadows and shapes and light and sounds and tastes and beauty so astounding it will make your head hurt.

Haney's photographs capture the sensibility of this place. And remind you again and again why you came here—and more importantly, why you're sure to come back.

Chris Peterson is a writer based in Columbia Falls, Montana. He spends about 200 days a year in Glacier National Park.

Above: A mountain goat kid, just a few weeks old, walks through a high-country meadow of glacier lilies. A favorite food for mountain goats, the glacier lily is one of the first flowers to bloom when the snow begins to melt in the high country. By winter, this kid's coat will be full and lush, with long, course guard hairs that keep the animal warm and repel wind, rain, and snow.

Facing page: Common and tenacious, arnica clings to the sheer cliffs of Rockwell Falls in Glacier's Two Medicine region. The falls is a popular stop for hikers en route to Cobalt Lake and Two Medicine Pass.

Above: A bighorn sheep ram strikes a stately pose against a backdrop of rocky peaks atop Logan Pass. During the summer, rams are a common sight at the pass. The park's rams form bachelor groups while the ewes raise the lambs on a separate summer range. In fall and winter, rams and ewes and their young come together in large herds.

Left: The fluffy white blossoms of bear grass grace the foreground of this view of Grinnell Lake. Bear grass is a member of the lily family, and the heads are actually hundreds of white flowers clustered together. About every three to ten years, the plants bloom en masse. Grinnell Lake gets its striking blue color from "glacier flour": rock ground up into fine particles by Grinnell Glacier, which feeds the lake. The hike to Grinnell Glacier is one of the most popular in the park. The mileage varies, depending on whether one shortens the trip by taking boats across Swiftcurrent and Josephine Lakes, but it generally takes most of the day if done entirely on foot.

Above: Glacier National Park was established in 1910, and the Great Northern Railway opened the Glacier Park Lodge in 1913 just outside the park in East Glacier. The massive timbers in the lobby are Douglas-fir, estimated to be between 500 and 800 years old. The railroad built all the major lodges inside Waterton Lakes and Glacier national parks.

Right: Sunrise casts golden light on the Glacier Park Lodge. The lodge is just a short walk from the East Glacier train station. Lodge staff take great pains to keep the gardens blooming throughout the summer months. The lodge is closed in winter.

Left: Camas, biscuitroot, and American bistort bloom in a Many Glacier meadow flanked by aspens. The edible bulb of the camas, the purple flower pictured here, was an important food source for several American Indian tribes.

Facing page: A triple waterfall cascades into Reynolds Creek at Logan Pass as the sun rises over the shoulder of Piegan Mountain.

Below: Fireweed blooms on the flanks of Glacier's Garden Wall as morning sun strikes Mount Oberlin and Mount Cannon. Glacier's Highline Trail takes visitors to this scene as it runs along the Continental Divide from Logan Pass to Waterton Lake.

Left: Autumn shows its teeth on a chilly morning at Bowman Lake.

Right: Amid a blaze of fall color, a stream tumbles down the ancient rocks of Mount Cannon toward the valley floor.

Below: A red bus crosses the St. Mary Bridge on an autumn day. The bus drivers are known as "jammers," as in gear jammers, because the original buses had manual transmissions, and grinding the gears was not uncommon while driving the Going-to-the-Sun Road. The Glacier "reds" began appearing in the park around 1935 and carried passengers for the next sixty years. The vintage buses have since been over-hauled and modernized, returning to the roadways in 2002.

Above: Mount Edwards and Gunsight Mountain glow in the winter evening light as a front blows over the Continental Divide. Gunsight is a popular mountain climb. The first known ascent was by early explorer Dr. Lyman Sperry in 1905.

Left: Glacier's southern end is true wilderness. Trails here are primitive, there are no roads, and you have to walk across the Middle Fork of the Flathead to access the landscape. On a bitterly cold winter evening, the river, which is normally a torrent, is subdued by frigid temperatures. At left is Mount Doody, with Wolftail Mountain at right.

Below: Cross-country skiers glide through a tunnel of snow-covered aspen. The average annual snowfall at park headquarters near West Glacier is 137.5 inches.

Above: One of Glacier's most popular destinations for hikers is Granite Park Chalet. The Great Northern Railway built the chalet in 1914–1915 as a backcountry hotel. Most visitors get to Granite Park by parking at Logan Pass and hiking the Highline Trail about eight miles to the chalet; the return trip can be shortened to four miles by hiking back down to the Going-to-the-Sun Road via the Loop Trail.

Right: Bear grass blooms along the trail at Logan Pass, as viewed east of the Continental Divide. At left is the distinctive horn of Mount Reynolds, and on the right is Mount Clements.

Above: The setting sun strikes low clouds on the flanks of Mount Wilbur, a prominent peak at Many Glacier. Although not the highest peak in the park at 9,321 feet, it is a challenging climb, with many treacherous cliffs.

Left: Bright-purple sticky geranium blooms on the prairie of the Blackfeet Nation, with Glacier's Chief Mountain in the distance. The mountain holds spiritual significance for several American Indian tribes. Its unique shape and prominence also drew the affection of early explorers. The mountain is "a worthy sovereign of any man's allegiance," remarked climber Henry L. Stimson in an essay on summiting the peak in 1892.

Above: Mottled brown plumage during the summer allows the white-tailed ptarmigan to blend in with its surroundings. In winter, the bird will turn completely white.

Left: Dawn paints the landscape around Marias Pass in pastel hues. The large peak at left is Calf Robe. Marias is a low pass (just 5,213 feet) over the Continental Divide. Despite bordering U.S. Highway 2 and the railroad, this area sees far fewer visitors than other regions of the park.

Below: Water spills over the top of Rockwell Falls. Glacier has 1,514 miles of perennial streams.

Right: Just 1.2 miles from the Going-to-the-Sun Road on Glacier's east side, St. Mary Falls is a popular stop for hikers.

Below: Huckleberries are a summer staple in Glacier. They're an important food source for birds and bears, and a nice snack for the hungry hiker.

A rainbow arcs above Swiftcurrent Lake and the Many Glacier Hotel. The hotel is the largest in the park, with five stories and 214 guest rooms. Like the other hotels in the park, it was built by the Great Northern Railway. The hotel opened to the public on July 4, 1915.

Right: At Many Glacier, canoes are stacked at the dock on mirror-like Swiftcurrent Lake. At right is Grinnell Point. In the distance is the distinct slope of Mount Gould and the Garden Wall.

Below: The Going-to-the-Sun Road is a popular destination for bicyclists, particularly in the spring when the road is closed to vehicles but open to hikers and cyclists. Here a pair on bikes rides through a section known as the Weeping Wall, where snowmelt cascades off Haystack Butte and down to the highway.

Above: An immature bald eagle surveys the landscape. Eagles are year-round residents in the park, particularly west of the divide, where streams continue to flow during winter.

Left: An aspen grove in peak fall colors. Aspens are a key species in the park. The young trees provide browse for moose, deer, and elk. The older trees, with their holes and little nooks, are perfect for nesting birds.

Below: A band of coyotes hunts the edge of a meadow near East Glacier. Coyotes are common in Glacier despite the presence of wolves, which will kill them if given the opportunity.

Above: Riding a bike over the Going-to-the-Sun Road is an experience like no other. Here, cyclists ride on the east side of the park.

Right: Sunrise gilds Chief Mountain, which casts a shadow on the smaller Ninaki and Papoose mountains to the southwest. In the distance at left is Gable Peak. Chief Mountain is an isolated remnant of the geologic formation known as the Lewis Overthrust. The surrounding rock has eroded away over the eons, leaving the mountain we see today.

Above: Lenticular clouds, named for their lens-like appearance, reflect in St. Mary Lake at sunset.

Left: Clouds hang low over Longknife Peak, on the north shore of Kintla Lake.
The peak straddles the border between British Columbia and Montana.

Below: The train depot at East Glacier isn't as busy today as it was in the heyday of the Great
Northern Railway, but many visitors, looking to relax and enjoy a trip to the park, come to
East Glacier on the Amtrak train, taking the same route of travelers more than 100 years ago.
The depot was completed in 1912, and the town was first called Glacier Park Station.
In 1950, the name was changed to East Glacier Park. The Glacier Park Lodge is across
Highway 49 from the depot.

Above: A billy mountain goat pauses for a portrait at Logan Pass. The affable creatures are a Glacier icon. Recent studies have shown the mountain goat population in the park is between 1,700 and 2,300 animals.

Right: Fog settles on Lake McDonald on a subzero winter afternoon. With a depth of 465 feet and a length of 9.4 miles, the lake is the largest in the park.

Left: Cataract Creek's Hidden Falls in the Many Glacier Valley is a nice stop for hikers on their way to Grinnell Lake or Piegan Pass.

Below: The Columbian ground squirrel is a common sight in Glacier in the summertime. They live throughout the park, from the valley floors to the highest passes, like this one gathering grass at Logan Pass. The squirrels breed, raise young, and fatten up all in the course of three to four months. The rest of the time they hibernate in deep burrows.

Above: Sunrise illuminates Mount Reynolds as a stream tumbles down Logan Pass.

Right: Wildflowers bloom along the shore of Swiftcurrent Lake as first light strikes Grinnell Point. The point, the mountain behind it, a glacier, waterfalls, and a lake are all named after George Bird Grinnell, an author and naturalist, editor of the magazine *Field and Stream*, and champion for the creation of the park in the late 1800s and early 1900s. Grinnell lived to see Glacier become a national park, and he coined the park's nickname "Crown of the Continent."

Facing page: Aspen groves primarily are clones (genetically identical trees with one root system), and related trees all turn color at once. Here, they blaze in striking colors along Lower St. Mary Lake.

Below: Slow-growing lichens add to the dazzling array of colors on many of the park's cliffs.

Right: The wind creates unusual ice formations on St. Mary Lake.

Far right: Bundled up against the cold, kayakers ply the chilly waters at Bowman Lake up the North Fork of the Flathead River. To the right is the dome of Rainbow Peak, flanked by golden larch forests.

Below: Ready for the cold with his full winter coat, a billy mountain goat makes his way up Altyn Ridge in the Many Glacier Valley. Mountain goats spend winters on windswept ridges, slopes, and ledges, their thick coats turning away the brutal chill.

Right: The Belton Train Depot in West Glacier is more than just a stop for passengers, it is also home to the Glacier Natural History Association, a nonprofit that supports park programs through its sales of maps, books, and other items.

Facing page: The red flowers of the paintbrush adorn the shoreline of Lake Josephine. Many different paintbrush varieties bloom from the valley floors to high-country cliffs and ledges.

Below: Experience a simpler time by relaxing in one of the old rocking chairs on the back porch of Lake McDonald Lodge.

Above: Two climbers make the final pitch to the summit of Mount Reynolds near Logan Pass, one of the more popular climbing destinations in the park.

Facing page: Water carves a path through the moss-covered rocks of Avalanche Gorge.

Left: Pitamakan Lake and the Cut Bank Valley as seen from Pitamakan Pass. The Lake of the Seven Winds is the small upper lake. The Dawson–Pitamakan hike is a popular loop in the park—just under nineteen miles from the Two Medicine campground and back. Many travelers split the trip into two or even three days, but particularly fit hikers often go light and knock it off from sunrise to sunset.

Below: Wild Goose Island is one of the most photographed subjects in the park. The name is derived from an occasional pair of geese thought to nest there.

Left: An American coot glides through a pond at Marias Pass. Coots are more commonly seen in large, black flocks on Lake McDonald in the spring as they migrate through the park.

Right: Reynolds Creek tumbles off cliffs near Logan Pass, which was named after William R. Logan, the first superintendent of the park.

Below: Framed by cottonwoods and aspens, the Going-to-the-Sun Road winds its way toward the Continental Divide on a clear autumn day.

Above: Apikuni Creek cascades to the valley floor at Many Glacier.

Left: Autumn in Glacier is a fickle affair: one minute there can be brilliant sunshine, the next a snow squall. Here, McDonald Creek and the Garden Wall glow in the last light of the day. The Garden Wall gets its name from a popular song in the 1890s, "Over the Garden Wall."

Above: The harlequin duck is a small sea duck that spends its life on the Pacific Coast, migrating inland to places like Glacier National Park in the spring to mate and raise young. McDonald Creek is a favorite nesting area for these unique and beautiful ducks.

Right: McDonald Falls throws off a haze of steam as temperatures drop to 20 degrees below zero on a brisk morning in Glacier.

Left: East of the Continental Divide there is generally a brisk wind, or at least a light breeze. But occasionally the skies go still, making for a perfect reflection of Grinnell Point in Swiftcurrent Lake.

Below: Completed in 1930, the Ptarmigan Tunnel is the only trail tunnel in the park. It allows for travel through the Ptarmigan Wall and connects the Many Glacier Valley with the Belly River country.

Following pages: A panoramic view of Triple Divide Pass. Water falling on Triple Divide Peak, in the background to the right, ultimately drains into the Pacific Ocean, the Atlantic Ocean, and Hudson Bay.

Right: Deep in the Belly River country is Dawn Mist Falls, a spectacular waterfall en route to Elizabeth Lake.

Below: This thimbleberry flower will form a bright-red thimbleberry —a tart and tasty treat along many of Glacier's low-elevation trails.

Above: With the thousands of visitors to Logan Pass each year, a boardwalk is necessary to protect the delicate vegetation. It also provides an easy route up the slope to the Hidden Lake Overlook, 1.5 miles up the trail.

Left: Scorched by several years of fires, Glacier's North Fork region is a mix of regenerating forests—some of the most diverse habitat in the park. Here, the high peaks reflect in a small pond at McGee Meadow.

Above: Aspens arrow their way skyward on a sunny fall afternoon.

Right: A dusting of snow on the Garden Wall accentuates Glacier's fall palette. It can snow any month of the year in the park, and snow generally begins to accumulate in mid-October, limiting access to Logan Pass to just a few short summer months.

Above: A full moon rises above the Cloudcroft Peaks in Glacier's southern region.

Left: All is still and quiet on Lake McDonald at dawn.

Right: A tour boat cruises Upper Waterton Lake. In Glacier, many services are located outside the park; however, in Waterton Lakes National Park, the Waterton townsite, including a golf course, sits inside the park's boundaries.

Far right: Hiking and climbing in Glacier can offer a fresh perspective on familiar landmarks, as in this view of the Many Glacier Hotel and Swiftcurrent Lake from the slopes above.

Below: In summer, mule deer roam the park's high alpine terrain. A buck sporting velvet antlers makes his way across a meadow at Logan Pass.

Left: A bird's-eye view of Iceberg Lake in the Many Glacier Valley. Glacier has more than 730 miles of trails, and one of the more popular hikes is the Iceberg Lake Trail in Many Glacier. The trail guides hikers about five miles to a lake at the base of Mount Wilbur that in the summertime is often full of large chunks of ice—thus the name.

Below: Visitors take in the views from a red bus along Glacier's Weeping Wall on the Going-to-the-Sun Road.

Above: Dew clings to prairie smoke wildflowers.
The feathery plumes give the plant its descriptive name.

Right: In a phenomenon known as alpenglow, a spectacular sunrise reflects
on storm clouds and peaks surrounding St. Mary Lake and Wild Goose Island.

Left: Autumn sunrise stains Yellow Mountain and the clouds above it a warm pink. Although Glacier's rocks are millions of years old, the park does see earthquakes. One tremblor resulted in Slide Lake—created when part of Yellow Mountain slid and dammed Otatso Creek. Today there is a most pleasant backcountry campground at the lake.

Below: The fireplace in the lobby of Many Glacier Hotel keeps visitors warm on cool summer mornings.

Right: The North Fork of the Flathead River originates deep in British Columbia. It flows for nearly fifty miles before entering Montana. Fed by snowmelt, the river runs cold and clear.

Below: The full moon rises over the Cloudcroft Peaks, pink with alpenglow.

Above: The hoary marmot, named for its silver-tipped hair, is a common species in Glacier's high country. Like the Columbian ground squirrel, it spends most of the year in hibernation.

Left: Travelers head up the Going-to-the-Sun Road. Completed in the fall of 1932 and opened to the public the next summer, the road, with its intricate stonework, arches, and bridges, is a National Historic Landmark.

Below: Crews begin plowing the Going-to-the-Sun Road in early April. It usually takes about three months to completely clear the road.

Right: Running Eagle Falls at Two Medicine was formerly known as Trick Falls. When water levels drop, a second waterfall is revealed beneath the first.

Below: A close-up view reveals the hundreds of individual flowers that make up a head of bear grass. American Indian tribes of the region wove bear grass leaves into baskets.

Above, top: Visitors to Glacier's North Fork would be remiss to not stop at the Polebridge Mercantile. The small store just outside the park has served the North Fork community for more than 100 years and has a renowned bakery.

Above: The view from inside the Numa Ridge Fire Lookout Tower high above Bowman Lake. Glacier still maintains and staffs several fire lookouts in the park, including Numa, Swiftcurrent, Huckleberry, and Scalplock. There is also a lookout tower on Mount Brown, but it is unstaffed.

Left: Kintla Lake is meant to be a quiet place. No boats with motors are allowed on its pristine waters.

Following page: Jackson Creek rushes through cedars not far from Lake McDonald Lodge. Glacier marks the western boundary of the red cedar, which thrives in the moist, temperate climate along Lake McDonald.